# FIXING BROKEN TRUSTS

## Heggstad and Trust Modification Petitions in California

Robert P. Bergman, Esq.

Jacobs & Whitehall
73-03 Bell Blvd, #10
Oakland Gardens, NY 11364
www.jacobsandwhitehall.com

Ordering Information:

Quantity sales. Special discounts are available on quantity purchases by corporations, associations, and others. For details, contact the publisher at the address above.

Orders by U.S. trade bookstores and wholesalers. Please contact Jacobs & Whitehall: Tel: (888) 991-2766 or visit www.jacobsandwhitehall.com.

Printed in the United States of America

Published in 2020

**ISBN:** 978-1-951149-34-5

# DISCLAIMER

This publication is intended to be used for educational purposes only. No legal advice is being given, and no attorney-client relationship is intended to be created by reading this material. The author assumes no liability for any errors or omissions or for how this book or its contents are used or interpreted, or for any consequences resulting directly or indirectly from the use of this book. For legal or any other advice, please consult an experienced attorney or the appropriate expert, who is aware of the specific facts of your case and is knowledgeable in the law in your jurisdiction.

**Law Offices of Robert P. Bergman**

Building Two
3535 Ross Avenue
Suite 308
San Jose, California
(408) 247-0444
www.lawbob.com

RPB Estate Planner
*Law Offices of Robert P. Bergman*

# Table of Contents

# About The Author

I was born in Tripoli, Libya to an Italian mother and then adopted by an American Air Force officer and his family. After traveling across the ocean on an ocean liner, I arrived in the United States where my father was stationed at an Air Force base in Michigan. Later, we moved to an Air Force base in Colorado Springs, Colorado, where I became a citizen at the age of four and a half. For years, we moved around to various Air Force bases in Bermuda and Virginia. In 1968, my father retired from the Air Force and moved the entire family to Silicon Valley, where I have lived ever since.

My original intention was to be a high school history teacher, and although I still have a love of history, that is not the kind of teaching I do now. During my senior year of college, I decided to pursue a law degree and eventually received my Juris Doctor from Santa Clara University School of Law.

I did not set out to study estate planning in law school, and it wasn't until I was working with a small firm in San Jose that I was even introduced to the topic. Through my firm, I began doing seminars on living trusts. After leaving that firm, I continued doing seminars and would estimate that throughout the course of my career, I've done 300 to 400.

I still do several seminars every year out of my office in San Jose, and there is a version of my living trust seminar on my YouTube channel The Law Offices of Robert P Bergman. A few years ago, that seminar went viral and has well in excess of 50,000 views.

A number of years ago, I became a board-certified specialist in estate planning, probate, and trust law through the California State Bar Board of Legal Specialization. This places me among a small number of attorneys in California that specialize in estate planning as opposed to just dabbling in estate planning.

## *A Member Of WealthCounsel For Over 10 Years*

WealthCounsel®

Practice Excellence.™

MEMBER 10+ YEARS

WealthCounsel is a national association of estate planning attorneys and other professionals, dedicated to providing the highest quality estate planning counseling and documentation for their clients.

## *What Did You Write This Book?*

I decided to write this book because I have found that there are likely thousands of families each year in the state of California that need to go to court to fix a broken trust of some kind—whether it's to change the terms of the trust to avoid having to take actions that are no longer necessary or appropriate, make modifications to the trust to provide more protection for heirs and beneficiaries, or gather loose assets into the trust that should've been there before the creator of the trust had died.

For those who live in one of several of the counties here in California (especially Southern California), the court process to fix broken trusts can be very expensive and take months to accomplish. I have a process that can often resolve issues in one to two weeks instead of months, and at a much lower cost than a family may suffer in other parts of the state.

I would like the readers of this book to come away with an appreciation that the situation that they may be facing is not unique, that there are solutions to their broken trusts, and that I can be the "doctor" with the remedy.

### *Who Is This Book For?*

This book is for anyone who is faced with the situation of a broken trust. This might be the successor trustee of a trust where a spouse, parent, another relative, or friend has died, or it might be the attorney helping a successor trustee of a trust who practices in the county where getting a broken trust fixed is a long, expensive process.

It might be a title or escrow officer faced with a new escrow for the sale of real estate where it is discovered that the real estate is not titled properly in the name of the trust of the original owner, and so the escrow cannot proceed until that problem is fixed.

Alternatively, it could be for a situation wherein a trust is leaving property directly to a special needs person, but in a way that will cause that person to lose their income, health insurance benefits, and potentially their housing. Through the court system, there are solutions to these problems and many others.

## *About The "Irrevocable Trust Doctor" Service*

Irrevocable Trust Doctor
Fixing Broken Trusts

To assist families that are exploring whether an irrevocable trust can be successfully modified, I have created a dedicated website that answers frequently asked questions, provides guidance, and permits any interested party the ability to schedule a free consultation with me. The website is www.irrevocabletrustdoctor.com.

# Testimonial

*"Robert did an excellent job for my family. We had a probate issue in which assets were left outside a trust. We needed to file the Heggstad petition to see if the court would deem that the assets should have been in the trust, so we could avoid probate. He checked with the court to confirm that based on the circumstances it would likely be granted. None of the attorneys I spoke with mentioned doing this or gave me any idea of what our chances for success would be if we chose to move forward with the petition. Robert's fees were very reasonable and he got the work done in a very timely manner. I would highly recommend Robert based on my experience of working with him on this estate issue."*

*– Amit*

# CHAPTER 1

# TRUSTS

### *The Ultimate Goal Of A Proper Trust*

Ideally, an estate plan provides for the avoidance of conservatorship during someone's lifetime if they become incapacitated, and the avoidance of the complicated and expensive probate process after death. Having a comprehensive estate plan will provide for the quick, efficient, and orderly distribution of someone's property to their ultimate heirs.

## *Components That Make Up An Effective Trust*

A well-crafted estate plan will include a living trust to hold the ownership of most of the property. A specially crafted will be called a pour-over will is designed to direct any property not in a person's trust at their death to be turned over to the trust, often using the Heggstad petition.

The living trust will provide for successor trustees to take over the administration of the property in the trust after the incapacitation or death of the creator of the trust. Living trusts also provide for the distribution of property after death, including any special provisions for distributions to beneficiaries who are special needs persons, or distributions in trust to provide asset protection for the beneficiaries who are receiving the property. I call that type of trust planning "castle trust planning," because it essentially builds a castle wall around the inheritance to protect it from divorcing spouses, accidents, malpractice claims, and creditor claims that might come against a beneficiary in their lifetime.

The estate plan will also include a financial power of attorney to handle any assets that cannot be owned by the living trust, such as retirement plans, as well as deal with government agencies, the court system, and filing tax returns for the person if they are incapacitated.

An advance health care directive is also part of an estate plan and designates a person to make medical and health care decisions for the person if they are no longer able to communicate with their doctors. Closely related to the advance health care directive is a HIPAA authorization, which lists the individuals who would be granted access to information about the person's medical conditions and health status.

For a married couple, a marital property agreement is often included to clarify what property is owned by the marriage and what property might be individually owned by one spouse.

An estate plan might also include a certification of trust that gives summary information about the living trust that can be used when dealing with financial institutions, such as banks, brokerages, and title companies in the sale or purchase of the real estate.

Often, there is a general assignment of property to the trust, which should include property to be acquired in the future and will often list various categories of property in order to show the intention of the creator of the trust regarding property that should be owed by the trust. A schedule of assets that is regularly maintained showing what is owned by the trust is also very important in order to provide proof of intent after someone has died.

## *How Often To Revisit Estate Planning Documents? What To Look For To Prevent Problems After Death?*

Once an estate plan has been established, I generally advise my clients to have it reviewed every five years or so because the laws and planning considerations may change during that time. I recommend an immediate review if there has been a change in the family situation such as a birth, death, sudden increase or decrease in wealth, or change in the health status of a family member due to an accident or disease. The latter is especially important if someone develops special needs.

In addition to working at my estate planning practice which involves preparing foundational estate plans using living trusts, powers of attorney, and advance health care directives, I regularly assist clients of my own and other attorneys in California with fixing trust-based estate plans that are "broken."

A broken trust typically falls into one of two categories. The first type of broken trust is one that was set up several years ago and may have requirements to divide the trust property at the death of a spouse into two or more distinct portions. These trusts are called A-B trusts and often require a surviving spouse to divide the property owned by the trust at the death of the first spouse. Due to changes in the federal estate tax laws, these types of trusts are often obsolete and no longer valuable.

The second type of broken trust is one where the trust was created but various property belonging to the creator of the trust was never transferred into the ownership of the trust before that person died.

I regularly go to court to fix broken trusts and have been doing so for several years. As it currently stands, I have done about 70 of these court petitions, and I am now going to court typically four to six times a month.

# TESTIMONIAL

*"I am a real estate broker who was involved in a short-sale transaction. Just before final documents were to be signed to close Escrow, the seller passed away. The property was in a trust and did not name a successor trustee. With the short sale approval deadline date coming very quickly, we thought that after a year of working on this transaction it would all fall to pieces. Robert literally saved the day. He was able to have a beneficiary on the trust appointed to successor trustee extremely quickly due to his expertise (right in the middle of the Christmas season). Every attorney we had spoken to up until Robert had said that the process would take a few weeks or that it could not be done at all, but after speaking to Robert for a few minutes, we knew he was our man. Not only was Robert punctual and professional but very kind and treated our situation as a priority. I highly recommend Mr. Bergman."*

*– Nicholas*

# CHAPTER 2

# BROKEN TRUSTS

### *How Can Trusts Be "Broken"? What Does It Mean?*

There are basically two ways in which a trust can be broken, and I will deal with each one separately because the solutions are different.

The most common way that a trust can be broken is when someone dies and leaves one or more assets either titled in their individual name or payable to their probate estate. I regularly deal with personal residences that were either never transferred into the trust in the first place or were taken out of the trust to refinance the property and never transferred back.

Under such circumstances, many families in various parts of California are enduring long, complicated, and expensive court processes called probate in order to eventually get that property into the trust where it should've been all along. This is typically done using the pour-over will, and often involves a year or more in the court system before the court will finally sign an order putting the property into the trust so that it can be distributed according to the terms of the trust.

The Heggstad petition can be filed with the probate court as a way of requesting the court to sign an order declaring that the assets that were left out of the trust be turned over to the ownership of the trust without the utilization of the probate process.

In order to support the granting of a Heggstad petition, the probate court will want to see that there is written evidence of the intention of the trustor that those assets be owned by the trustor's trust. For example, if the trustor's residence was first transferred to the trust ownership but then taken out to refinance the mortgage, then the original transfer deed is good evidence of the intention that the trustor had the residence owned by the trust.

There may be a written schedule of assets attached to the trust that lists one or more of the assets, which is further written evidence of intent. There may be an assignment of personal property or another assignment of assets that identifies the type of assets, such as a checking account, brokerage account, or automobile intended to be owned by the trust.

There could even be a handwritten note or a letter from the trustor that identifies the asset in question. Another possibility is that the specific asset is mentioned in the trust itself as designated for a specific beneficiary. Given that the trust is signed by the trustor that would be pretty clear evidence of intent.

The other type of broken trust occurs most frequently with an older trust that was drafted for a married couple at a time when the federal estate tax exclusion amount was low compared to the exclusion amount today. This type of trust is generally called an A-B marital trust. For example, a trust that was drafted for a married couple in 1995 would reference an exclusion amount of $600,000 for each spouse. In the year 2020, the federal estate tax exclusion amount is $11.58 million and will be increasing over the next few years. Even if the current federal estate tax exclusion amount does not continue past its current expiration date, the exclusion amount in the future will be about half of the current exclusion.

Thousands of trusts drafted for married couples in the 1980s, 1990s, and 2000s require that the property in the trust be divided into shares when the first spouse dies. Today, the exclusion amount for each spouse is several million dollars.

## *How To Discover A Broken Trust? At What Point Do People Contact You?*

In my experience, a broken trust is generally discovered when an original creator of the trust dies. If the surviving spouse goes to an estate planning attorney right away to determine what needs to be done for the marital trust administration and the existence of an A-B marital trust is discovered during that meeting, then the surviving spouse will be in the position of either doing the trust administration and dividing the trust assets into two pieces or going to court with the consent of all of the beneficiaries to modify the trust and remove that requirement.

Unfortunately, after the death of the first spouse, many surviving spouses don't actually do anything with the trust, but instead, operate off the assumption that they own everything in the trust and that none of the beneficiaries could assert a legal claim against any part of the assets in the trust. I regularly consult with surviving spouses who either come into my office locally or are referred to me from other parts of the state where the first spouse died several years prior and administration was never done.

As a further complication, many attorneys are unaware of the legal consequences of not administering an A-B marital trust in the way it reads. In fact, I have encountered ignorant attorneys who amended the original trust at the directions of the surviving spouse without regard to the rights of the beneficiaries of the deceased spouse's share of trust property. I have also encountered attorneys who have tried to modify an A-B marital trust by having the surviving spouse and the remainder beneficiaries enter into a written agreement that no trust administration is necessary. Both approaches are wrong and can create legal problems for the surviving spouse or for the remainder beneficiaries of the deceased spouse.

An older trust might not contain provisions for a special needs beneficiary and may direct outright distribution of inheritance to such person. This is also a broken trust that needs to be fixed because a special needs person receiving an inheritance directly can end up losing all of the benefits that they are receiving from the government—including housing, health insurance, income, and access to much-needed programs for assistance.

The other type of broken trust is one that requires a Heggstad petition because there is at least one asset of the deceased creator of the trust that is in that person's name or payable to their estate after death. Unfortunately, this is often discovered when that person's home has been sold by the successor trustee and is already in escrow. It's only at that time that a preliminary title report is issued by the title company which shows that the property is, in fact, in the individual name of the trust creator and not in the name of the trust.

# TESTIMONIAL

*"Bob does a very nice job in walking the layman through the complexities of estate tax law as it currently exists, as well as providing insights on how it might change based on any pending legislation or the prevailing political climate. He uses a rigorous process for gathering detailed information on a client's financial and familial situation along with their long-term needs and desires. Using this process, he can quickly compile a comprehensive estate plan to address those needs while minimizing the tax exposure to the estate and to heirs. He also provides detailed written instructions and all the necessary forms to enable the client to expeditiously implement the resulting trust. Bob is very personable and easy to work with. I have referred several clients to him and they were all pleased with the results."*

*- Michael*

# CHAPTER 3

# LET'S FIX IT

### *Possible Remedies For Broken Trusts*

In my experience, when there is a broken trust and the creator of the trust has already died, the only remedy is to petition the probate court for a modification or termination of what has become a revocable trust. This type of petition is under California Probate Code Section 15403 or 15409 and involves filing a petition with the court that specifically identifies the modifications that are being requested. These modifications could include removing all references to dividing the trust assets into two or more new trusts because of the death of the first spouse, modifying the inheritance to be received by a special needs beneficiary so that it is directed into a supplemental needs trust for that person, or even adding distributions to other beneficiaries to eventually go into asset-protected trusts for them during their lifetimes.

In the case of an A-B marital trust that has already been divided into two trusts, the modification may involve granting a general power of appointment in favor of the surviving spouse to decide where the assets of the deceased spouse's irrevocable trust will eventually be distributed. The reason for doing this would be to cause the irrevocable trust property to be included in the taxable estate of the surviving spouse when the surviving spouse dies. This "estate inclusion" will cause that property to receive new capital gains "step up" on a cost basis at the death of the surviving spouse. The effect of that will be to make sure that the family does not pay capital gains income tax on the growth in the value of the deceased spouse's irrevocable trust from the time that the person dies to the date that the surviving spouse dies.

## *What Is The Heggstad Petition?*

The Heggstad petition requests that the court declare a property that is still in the name of the deceased creator of the trust, or payable to that person's estate as assets of the trust without going through the formal process of probate. Such an approach can also be used to take over property that someone else is holding that, in fact, is property of the deceased creator of the trust—the ultimate purpose being to have the court turn that property over to the trust.

## *Heggstad Petition And Requirements For A Successful Heggstad Petition*

Like any court petition, a Heggstad petition is drafted and submitted to an appropriate probate court for consideration. A successful Heggstad petition must provide written evidence that the creator of the trust intended for the property in the petition to be part of their trust either during their own lifetime or after their death. Evidence for this can include the following:

1. A prior transfer of real estate that changed the title to the trust ownership but was taken out of the trust to refinance a mortgage.
2. A schedule of assets of the trust that lists specific assets that were not retitled into the trust ownership during the creator's lifetime.
3. A general assignment of assets to the trust that lists specific categories of assets such as jewelry, real estate, automobiles, bank accounts, and brokerage accounts.
4. A statement in the trust itself that identifies the certain property as going to a specific beneficiary, such as a residence identified by its address or legal description.
5. Any other writing of the creator that shows the intention that certain property be owned by the trust.
6. In some counties in California, a special type of will called a pour-over will specifically indicate that any property subject to probate is to be turned over to the creator's trust after the creator has died.

## *When Can I File A Heggstad Petition?*

The Heggstad petition is usually filed after the creator of the trust has died but can be filed while that person is incapacitated if there is property of theirs that should be in the trust. A family might do this prospectively so that property is already owned in the creator's trust at his or her death and no further court action will be necessary.

### *How Long Does A Heggstad Petition Take?*

Working through my office, a Heggstad petition can be submitted to the court within 7 to 10 from time we are first contacted. However, it will be necessary for all the remainder beneficiaries of the trust to agree and sign a waiver of notice of the petition, consent to the petition, and consent to having the petition heard in the probate court.

### *Why Is A Heggstad Petition Better Than Probate?*

Using a Heggstad petition is much better than going through the probate process for several reasons, including the following:

1. The issue of loose assets can be resolved in a single day rather than eight or nine months to a year or more through the probate process.

2. The costs associated with probate and the extremely high statutory attorney fees can be avoided, potentially saving tens of thousands of dollars.
3. A family can take control of real property and get it sold right away instead of enduring months of having to make mortgage payments, property tax payments, insurance payments, utility payments, homeowner dues, and property maintenance.

# Testimonial

*"I cannot say enough good things about Robert Bergman. Recently, my family found itself in a real bind, following the unexpected death of my brother. For many years, my brother had used the services of a Bay Area estate attorney, periodically making changes to his trust. Upon his death and with the imminent sale of his property, we were faced with the unpleasant news that his trust was not, in fact, going to protect his assets. After all of the years of visiting and paying his attorney, it was all for naught!*

*Upon the recommendation of the probate court overseeing my brother's jurisdiction and a series of subsequent attorneys, we were advised to contact attorney Robert Bergman, who, though not located anywhere near my brother's property, was not only well-versed in our predicament and the reasons for it (which could easily have been avoided), but was able to quickly turn the situation around to our benefit, thus avoiding probate and allowing for the successful sale of the property. Had he not been so capable and expedient (time was of the essence!), I am convinced that the sale would have fallen through.*

*Robert Bergman is not only extremely knowledgeable and thorough but is especially kind and thoughtful. In my dreams and given our predicament, I did not expect to be placed in such capable hands! He is truly the man you want to assist with your estate planning and financial needs – THANK YOU, Bob!"*

*– Linda*

# CHAPTER 4

# WAIT – I THOUGHT TRUSTS CAN'T BE CHANGED

### *I Thought That An Irrevocable Trust Can't Be Changed. Isn't That Correct?*

While it was certainly true in the past that irrevocable trusts could not be changed, they may be one of the most revocable and amendable trusts that currently exist. This is because of Probate Code Sections 15403 and 15409.

## *Sections Of The California Probate Code That Permit Modification Of An Irrevocable Trust*

California Probate Code Sections 15403 and 15409 permit modification of an irrevocable trust after one or both creators of the trust have died. A third section, Probate Code 15404, permits the modification of an irrevocable trust if the original creator of the trust and all current beneficiaries of the trust agree in writing. However, this section of the probate code cannot be used when one of the original creators of a trust is already deceased.

## *When Can A Trust Not Be Modified After Someone Has Passed Away?*

There is no irrevocable trust that cannot be modified after the creator of the trust has died, except for those to which one or more beneficiaries oppose a proposed modification. If a proposed modification does not affect the rights of a beneficiary of the trust, it may still be possible to get the trust modified as to the rights of one or more beneficiaries that agree with the change.

# TESTIMONIAL

*"My wife and I attended one of Bob's seminars on estate planning. I was amazed at his knowledge and qualifications and the ability to explain the subject matter. We made an appointment and had him draw up a living trust for us. After a couple of appointments and some paperwork, we have a solid plan for our estate. Bob is also incredibly accessible and supportive after your plan is in place. I recently needed some information from him for my new job and he provided exactly what I needed in a voicemail immediately. I'm not used to that kind of turnaround from anyone.*

*I strongly recommend people do estate planning with Bob Bergman or at the very least, attend one of his seminars and talk to him and I think you'll be as impressed as we were."*

*- John H.*

# CHAPTER 5

# CHOOSING THE RIGHT ATTORNEY TO FIX YOUR TRUSTS

You have a great deal of experience in fixing broken trusts and the Heggstad petition. What specifically sets you apart in handling these matters for prospective clients?

- I handle the entire petition process personally;
- I hold an initial consultation with clients and/or their attorneys;
- I perform the drafting of the petition and necessary waivers and consents from the beneficiaries;

- I submit completed petitions directly to the court in person and obtain the signed court order the same day; and
- I return the order to the client or their attorney.

I call this my "white glove" service, and I pride myself on turning petitions around quickly and efficiently. To date, my record is a Heggstad petition that started on a Friday morning while talking with an attorney in Southern California who was involved with an escrow. The escrow could not be closed because the residence of the deceased trust creator was not in the trust ownership. The buyer in the escrow was about to lose his loan commitment, which would have led to the loss of the sale.

Working over the weekend, I drafted the petition and distributed the completed petition and waivers to the successor trustee and beneficiaries by email. I received everything back by Sunday night, and on Monday afternoon I obtained the court order turning over the residence to the trust ownership. I then overnighted the certified copy of the court order to the title company, and the sale was able to close.

## TESTIMONIAL

*"Bob Bergman has been our estate planning lawyer for many years and has also advised us numerous times when we needed other legal help. He has always been easy to work with, cheerful, and most importantly, his advice has always been "right on the mark." We value him both as a counselor and as a friend."*

*- Janice*

# INDEX

# NOTES

Made in the USA
Monee, IL
05 November 2026

67385056R00029